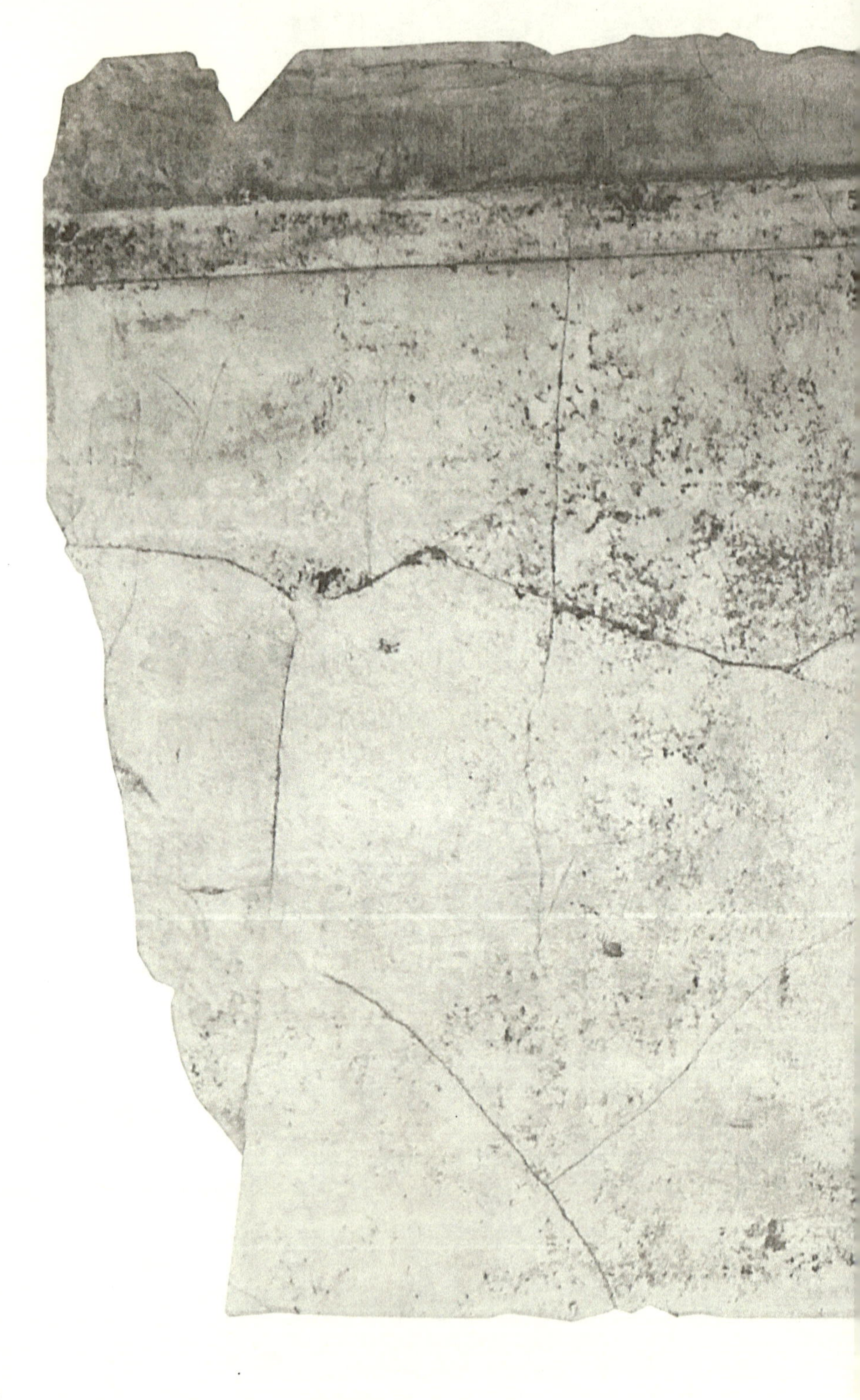

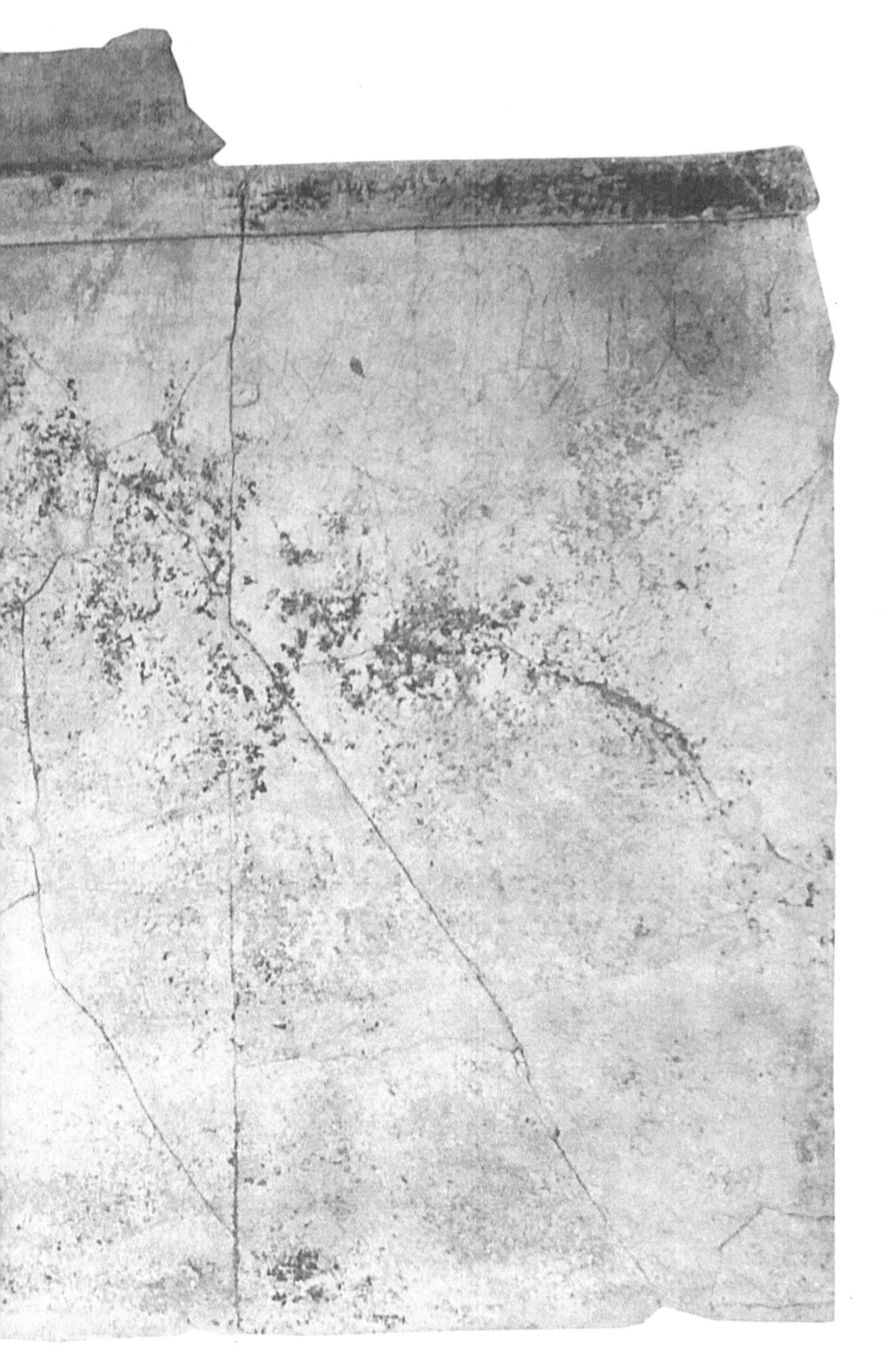

GABRIELE TINTI

Bleedings

Incipit Tragœdia

Translator

DAVID GRAHAM

Translator Editor

NICHOLAS BENSON

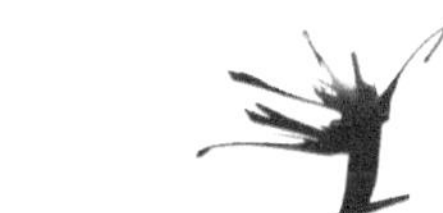

Contra Mundum Press New York · London · Melbourne

Bleedings — Incipit Tragœdia
© 2023 Gabriele Tinti &
David Graham

Cover image: *Blood Stream*
© 1987 Andres Serrano

First Contra Mundum Press
Edition 2023.

Library of Congress
Cataloguing-in-Publication
Data

Tinti, Gabriele, 1979–

Bleedings — Incipit Tragœdia /
Gabriele Tinti

—1st Contra Mundum Press
Edition
174 pp., 6 × 9 in.

ISBN 9781940625607

I. Tinti, Gabriele.
II. Title.
III. Graham, David.
IV. Translator.

2023933681

Table of Contents

30 No one feels pity
31 If you delve into the sea of absence
32 Speak to me again
33 Heavy in the bowels
34 I see myself after death
35 Like a farmer
36 Scratch the grave
37 No shelter
38 I won't stay long
39 Every effort takes me down
40 Forgive me
41 The sky falls onto you
42 Pale stone
43 You will follow me tomorrow
44 I get rid of the flesh
45 Who are you?
46 Nunc sum defleti parva favilla rogi
47 Follow me where everything gives way
48 I dreamt of this moment
49 You can no longer find the valve
50 Along the way
51 I free my arms
52 In a putrid latrine
53 I go all the way down
54 Drop by drop
55 In an inferno of hope
56 I blink my eyes
57 Unhappy mask
58 I would like to drink from your veins
59 To bleed
60 It is best
61 Try, if you can
62 I will sleep as I once did

96 A pool of mire
97 I ran away, hold me tight
98 The vein writhes
99 I sew the hemorrhage
100 You dig where there's no oxygen
101 Tempt fate
102 Miserable land
103 If I should die tonight
104 You flay the bark shelter
105 Something has gone wrong
106 In the stream of pulses
107 Open your eyes
108 This is the realm of the long shadows
109 Don't make me speak
110 Look at my yesterday's wound
111 Slumped in the scrub
112 I opened my body
113 The earth laughs at your fear of pain.
114 You put on your make-up at every change of scene
115 Facing the wall
116 I pay dearly
117 You will be remembered
118 Breathe water
119 I drag my bones
120 You are bruised
121 Out of focus
122 You sunk your hands into your ribs
123 I am trapped in the scene
124 Our tiers
125 The river has shaped a coffin
126 It's not worth it
127 I don't know how to go on
128 I'm not talking about you

129 Off camera
130 The memory trickles
131 You have brought me down here
132 Under the stone's feet
133 This is my body
134 Soiled with words I ruptured my veins
135 Why are you taking me away from this breath?
136 What else?
137 It will be all or nothing!
138 View without eyes
139 Your voice is counting down
140 This is how it will be

Bleedings

Incipit Tragœdia

Dear figure

Dear figure, do you really summon my song?
ἦ πεφόβησαι. 1

Terrenum corpus

Terrenum corpus, 2
it is memory, it weighs down.

Smeared with words
it wears away.

It is six foot three.
It is bottomless, it devours.

It comes from afar.
Made of light and shade.

It well knows that out there
there is more: a danger,

a curse,
a blessing.

It takes the road
it knows its end.

Down there the phantoms
become dust.

There is no choice but
to shorten one's step,

to grit one's teeth
to hone hope;

to not be content
with the bones.

The grass will grow from my breast

I will decay there with you, shrivel up defying fate.
I will chew what remains with my mouth full.

The grass will grow from my breast, it will plaster my hair,
let me drown in the noise of my ancestors.

King of the pools

King of the pools you wallow
in the ruins of words,

you knock into the loops of the veins,
sink into the soft bank

that wants you.

I go up to get hurt

I go up to get hurt
on this ancient hill,
full of faith in the horizon.
Sed quid ego hoc cerno? 3
The shadow of a yew
with branches stretched
around the neck,
ready to clench.
The sky sneers
a cruel quip,
the clouds show me
the direction of dawn.
I remain suspended
in this repetition
of days gone by,
of lost signs.

You hang paralyzed

You hang paralyzed
over the emptiness of the day.

You disturb the quiet
of ancient relics,

cut off your breath,
close your throat.

You throw open the door
of your beating bowels.

You have already had your share.

Ancient words breathe

Ancient words breathe,
they force you to listen.

It is late: your stomach
burns, your eyes throb.

Hec uia tale puluer habet. 4
Leave a sign there — you weigh down.

Infected by the tears
of the offended simulacra,

you can do nothing but go out
to quench your thirst.

Your step quickens, reopens
the wound, defiles the earth.

Better go back to the shelter
for a while, to forget.

This is no time to sleep

This is no time to sleep,
the rain is coming.

It will drizzle on the parched vein,
roll to the horizon,

quicken fate.

Please go

Please go ahead, towards the right,
towards the sacred woods of Persephone.

There you will lose your dizziness,
your violent songs, your idols.

You should have done so long ago,
but you chase dangerous fantasies,

you insist on wandering,
on laughing at the top of your voice,

on bleeding.

As you sink

As you sink stay with the bodies of the past.
You are foreign even to your dearest, an outcast,
a cold meal.

You fear the steps

You fear the steps of the punctured lives,
the engraved temples, the deformed

bodies.

You fear the strut
of that burnt torso,

the thrill of the needle,
the breath of the shadows.

You fear the solitude,
the smell of sadness,

the high choir of the graves.

Here we fired the shot

Here we fired the shot.

Plug my wound if you like,
inject the broth

you made ready,
that handful of words.

You'll close my eyes

You'll close my eyes,
you'll remember how it was,

you'll lead the way.

Don't leave my body to the dogs

Don't leave my body to the dogs,
burn it far away with its ills.

The fire will cleanse its wounds, the ashes
will soothe its challenges. At a thousand degrees

my bite will still be strong,
my sin, this comedy.

They would like to have locked me up

They would like to have locked me up
in an empty room, sedate me.

I opened a gap in the stone,
I puffed up my chest, released life.

I ruined my throat lighting up the night,
swept through forests, valleys, cities

only to fall,
to go a bit further on

— to sink.

Sometimes

Sometimes just one blow is enough,
a single blow to feel

the real source
of the pain.

The stone moves

The stone moves,
it seeks your eyes,
it covers the earth.

There is no longer anything
sprouting there,

nothing to show.

It's raining, as usual

It's raining, as usual.

The needle asks
to come in.

You clear the space
whatever it takes.

You need to stay
close to the blade,

at the mercy of pain.

The past shakes the corpses

The past shakes the corpses,
mixes the havens, directs the instincts.

It is voracious, burns with hunger,
changes its voice, insinuates doubt.

It has come to find me,
to close my eyes, my bowels, my future.

It pushes at the gates of desire,
draws my prints.

It walks fast, reflects
the disaster, prepares the pallet.

Tired of being body

Tired of being body
you'll find me lying flat
struggling with shadows:
fatuous fire, breath counted.

In the furrow of words

In the furrow of words
I sense a new voice.

Yearning for the future
I shoot yet another line

— always that one.
In the stone facades

blow for me the music
of the night. It is close.

I could listen to
its snares, its deceptions

instead I waste away
in the space opened up

by thc old light,
I look away.

Stick to the subject

Stick to the subject
tighten your grip, despite
everything feel again thirsty for time,
don't concede to exhaustion.

Eyes of stone

Eheu! Much diminished, I bare my bones, 5
I growl a sad verse to lighten the torment.

Those stony gazes long for me,
they preserve the voices for new songs.

I make the most of them, keep vigil, brighten,
I steal a sign in the moonlight.

The road rushes towards
the square. I follow it with eyes

closed, with one last chord,
I turn the stomach, I sink.

Fantasies bleed among these remains.
It is the old game that repeats, that returns.

They are carving the flesh

They are carving the flesh
they cling with the forceps
to the throbbing brain.
They curse. They pull.
My body howls to the world:
aliquoties natus sum,
set sic nunquam. 6

I made my coffin ready

I made my coffin ready, in the thud of evening.
I was mirrored in it, I found my way back.

I'm through with that, I want only to lose myself
in the noise of the city, in the light that confounds,

in the pain that digs.

The wind beats under the door

The wind beats under the door,
crosses the room, caresses

the days-old corpse.
It will soon flourish in a breath of grass,

out of sight.

Water trickles into the casket

Water trickles into the casket
devours the body of stone.

It seeps into the chambers,
filters, chills.

It falls, roars,
rises to the throat.

Don't you have the courage
to look?

You're trembling, hurry up,
turn the corner.

Innuis et negitas?
Tamen hoc redeudus tibi. 7

I cover my eyes and mouth with my hands

I cover my eyes and mouth with my hands
to better sing the emptiness of my bones.

I am waiting for someone to knock on the door,
something different, a new start.

I pour the shadow into a phial,
I lick away the blood from my veins,

that ancestral blood that drips
and shakes the words.

I would like

I would like to end up far away
from the foul smell of burials,
to flatten myself in the cage of duration,
fall there where no one can find me.

I can't do any more

Iam iam
cito cito, 8
I breathe deeply
I can't do any more.
It won't be long now:
the relics are withering
the past is pressing
my body responds
with pain.

No one feels pity

No one feels pity
for you, for a specter.

Life killed you quickly,
You passed in a moment.

What do you think your name means
down there? It is a craving extinguished

in the pallor of a stone face,
a mea culpa recited to the earth.

If you delve into the sea of absence

If you delve into the sea of absence
you'll find a fasting oracle.

It awaits you there, it pities you.
Its eye tolls in mourning,

it sees, plunges, attracts you.
With bitter voice it stabs

a curse, it twists
a handful of mysteries,

draws the vision.

Speak to me again

Speak to me again — you beg me —
but my heart shines in the shadow.

My mouth is leaden
heavy in its empty shelter,

singing in silence.

Heavy in the bowels

The throats of the ankles
open up, they are thirsty.

I give them a drink
a broth of bile.

The flesh is weak,
it is losing ground.

The ancient auguries
muddle the way,

they open the flank,
they wound the voice.

Heavy in the bowels
the memory of the end,

of the pain that kills,
of the earth that covers.

I see myself after death

I see myself after death:
the empty cortege wanders
nailing a coffin
of snow. The wailing
of the bells
will waken the respects,
the handshakes,
the small boat
that founders
in the grass.

Like a farmer

Like a farmer I plough the same page;
stubbornly repeat the pointless rite of sacrifice.

I go down towards the ditch, towards an end
that is not there, that I don't find. I stretch

my arms, raise my head, dig in my heels
to push my cart a little further on.

I know how to do it but I would really like only
to stop, to bend my knees, to rest.

Scratch the grave

Scratch the grave where they have enclosed you,
engrave the walls with your fingernails, try to escape.

Move the air with your hand, lick your wounds.
Check your teeth worn by the time spent

clenching them to protect you from yourself,
from the promises.

No shelter

No shelter:
greedy blades

have sprouted
from my infected breast.

Wash away this abomination
if you feel like it,

stitch the wound,
treat fate.

I won't stay long

I won't stay long
with my eyes upturned
gnashing my teeth
shaking my arms
frothing with chimeras.

Every effort takes me down

Te, lapis, optestor leviter super ossa residas. 9
My face is already macerated, my flesh rotted.

I anoint it with myrrh, get it ready.
My breath is broken, my throat wheezes.

Every effort takes me down.

Forgive me

Forgive me
if I am defenseless,
if I am always in pain,
if I cling to the grave
of my sinking body.

The sky falls onto you

The sky falls onto you
tears the air from your lungs,

throws you into a bottomless pit.
One after the other the ink

drops falls, spreads.

Pale stone

Invenies titulo nomina fixa meo,
my masks, my melodrama.

I am an open sore in the ruin
of a spectral temple, a pale stone.

You will follow me tomorrow

You will follow me tomorrow, on the brink of fate
we will sink together, hand in hand.

I would like such a death, a maternal sorrow
but the journey is uncertain, it falls in the lane.

The will grasps to new remnants,
another mirage.

I get rid of the flesh

I get rid of the flesh.
My blood ripples in a pool,
my bones swagger through the tall grass,
my words founder in the struggle.

Who are you?

Pis: tiú:
Íív: kúru: 11
with too much memory
— a heap.
You would like to throw me
to the bottom of the sea,
make me disappear.
I know, I'm a burden to you,
I don't let you sleep.
Throw me away,
it doesn't matter where.
I'll find my port,
I'll be able to endure.

Nunc sum defleti parva favilla rogi 12

Always in step, always taut
like an irascible string

stuffing myself with you
down in the graves.

Follow me where everything gives way

Follow me where everything gives way
where life burns brightly and fades.

Plunge with me into this sleepless
night, swollen with thoughts.

Pour the spirit into the mat.
Come in. Close the door.

Try to die.

I dreamt of this moment

I dreamt of this moment:
a desert of remains, the night
that never ends, the times passed,
a pistol at my temple,
a part that appears,
my body that disappears.

You can no longer find the valve

You can no longer find the valve
open in the arms.

In the pockets of veins
you seek it with the tip,

trace the scars
on the parched skin,

sniff out the source that
finally bursts,

throbs, overflows,
indulges you.

Along the way

Along the way I hurt myself,
my spirit weakened, I fell.
If you can facitis vobis suaviter,
et ego canto. 13

I free my arms

I free my arms:
I no longer want to go down
where the road ends.

In a putrid latrine

In a putrid latrine,
you lay, among flowers and candles,

your helpless body,
with the photo beside,

shrouded by the obscene breath
of that steel table.

I go all the way down

I go all the way down:
shattered glass,

sack of verses,
yearning for tragedy.

Drop by drop

Drop by drop the silence trickles,
turns into a river, a current that leaps

against your crushed head,
your little paper palace.

In an inferno of hope

In an inferno of hope
may tomorrow be like this moment,

may it return the same. Our feet
are ready for the road.

It would be better not to speak,
put the earth in focus,

plunge into the fray.

I blink my eyes

Admiror, o pariens, te non cecidisse ruinis
before these attacks, my voice. 14

I blink my eyes, I see: nothing diverts them
from the stain of the obituaries, the corteges.

There must be something behind those photos:
a shadow of the ancient tumult, a gathering.

Unhappy mask

Unhappy mask
under this light
sing rambling
in the wake of summer
from the ground that opens up.

I would like to drink from your veins

I would like to drink from your veins,
in long swigs, as one should.

From mouth to mouth you traced
the way, the last pretense,

nostalgia.

To bleed

Eundum est tamen. 15
Though where, I do not know, and yet one must.

I put my bones on top of one another,
I get ready. Something impels me

to breathe where others don't want to
— to bleed. I'll go without shelter.

I'll go out courting my umpteenth
feat, the tip of a needle.

It is best

It is best
to bring it on

do it now.
For the whole night

I have pricked
my ankles.

My dark rings
light up

my step trembles.
In the pillage of the remains

I put my hand
on the holster,

the aim lost.

Try, if you can

Coge mori, 16
try, if you can.

Take a stand,
turn off the light.

My head drips,
it is in turmoil.

It has no time
for surrender.

I will sleep as I once did

I will sleep as I once did
in the hot breath of the hemorrhage.

I will dream of the immense shadow
of an ancient stone falling.

I will cling to that heap
of dust, I will not want to waken.

Mission complete

Mission complete:
I burn my throat,
my wrists tremble,
I go forth and back.

Corrupted by the past

Corrupted by the past, I heard the marble breathe.
I burnt a fistful of words for that urn.

Nothing will distract me from the ruins
ravaged by cement, by the crutches of here in time.

Postin viam videtas t<i>t<e>s tokam alies
Esmen vepses vepeten, sleeping rough, 17

without shelter. Hold your tongue
full of oblivion, of falsehoods; be quiet.

Listen to the bells: they come down from Santa Maria,
they sing for us, they recognized us by the smell.

I would like to step aside

I would like to step aside,
make things easier,

leave off dying
for a few words

I would like to take refuge,
play fair and square,

escape the impediment
of my leaden body.

The yew keeps watch

The yew keeps watch stuck amongst the garbage.
Inscribed in the ribs of the tomb it rises

out of the clod, it weighs on the stone.

You feed on lies

You feed on lies, on pride in your voice.
Every time you stumble into the new day,

you go down into the abyss.
Look for asylum down there:

follow a sign, taste the earth.
You're avid for the current, the depths.

You're a swollen body. Never go back.
You were born to languish, to mumble

foreign words, to fade.

Your deceptions are lost in the shadows

Your deceptions are lost in the shadows,
They pile up in the garbage.

You prowl like flame, you love the syringe.
With every breath you get smaller, move away.

Four blocks further on is a piece of land,
some chrysanthemums, thousands of you in a casket.

One final count

One final count of the bones as
the light recedes. Lick the vision,

challenge the anathema. The grass safeguards
the stylish body bag, that little truce.

In the middle

Culter sinistrorsum, culter dextrorsum 18
and us in the middle, with so little to say.

Bring the spikes

Bring the spikes, come close, make yourself comfortable.
I'll offer you my veins, we'll make the earth shake.

Don't leave me

Don't leave me. Hell digs into my blood.
I stumble, I strive; I have not yet learnt to be here.
Teach me how, stop the bleeding, fight for me.

Prodigal son

I will meet you in the morning,
in front of the museum, where
you never thought to take me.

I will recognize you in an ancient
stone face, and I will want
to hold you close

in the embrace that you and I,
after all, never had.
And together we will lower our gaze

so as not to see in the eyes the horror
of time passed too quickly,
to finally think of something else.

Gladiators

We had fun improvising
to make the time pass for them.

We nailed that torso to the corner
beating it till it bled.

We used up all our energy
in this decrepit setting.

Flee? Where could we go?
The autumn is dusty,

there are few breaks.
The bodies leave no trace.

Our spirits fly off stealthily,
without being noticed,

while the bench leaps
in a moment and life adheres

to these teeming gestures
and reflections, to this struggle.

The seer

After having sung so long I have lost my voice.
Beggar beneath the Mole, worn down by so many disappointments, 19
I am closed up in myself, in this gallery full of shadows,
of discharge, of dereliction. I have just discovered that

there is someone here with me. I cannot understand who it is
and the anguish keeps me awake. I have no reason for it, after all
no one is looking for me, no one expects me. They scorned
my desire for the impossible, the overturning of things,

of every surface. They did it to confine me to a corner
because 'there is no reason to feed a seer.'
That's what they say and how it is. I will put nothing aside,

nothing that may soothe their wounds.
Only to that shape will I tell the new life.

The Song of love

This perfect day may return.
I heard it whisper in a song of love

murmured in a low voice by the painter.
But in the dark cavities of a portico

I saw Apollo lose his head.
They stuck it on the wall

of a whimsical wing. He looked at me from there,
with tender eyes, of stone. What nostalgia!

They betrayed, scorned, forgot him.
The fatal sound of his voice, lost.

I long suffered and wept for him
but my heart is weary, it has had enough.

For now make do with this cloudless sky,
jump on board and say your prayers.

Soon a new poet will be born with forceps,
he will ambush death to better observe it.

He will wager against himself, against you, and free
the god from that torment in which you have hung him.

And we will go back to playing without concerns,
to laughing at the night, at the words.

Polyphemus

Barbarian without hope
indulge your fate.

Suck the flesh you reprobate,
no one will come to your aid.

They leave you intoxicated in pieces,
smothering your sight. Do you hear them?

The getaway is already distant,
it rustles leaving no trace.

What a trap they set for you!
They roll on their backs.

They laugh! They laugh! They clap their hands!
You curse toward the new sun,

you suffer insensate, you damn them,
you fall lost, in the belly of the morning.

Say no more

Say no more, quench yourself
from these veins opened for you,

from my ravenous breath.
What would you like me to sing this evening?

Cruel inspiration strikes.
At times I arouse fear, I know.

My smell is strong, it is of the earth.
Do not be afraid, let yourself go

in my verses, take your place; life is here,
it will fulfill every promise, every self-conceit.

Why are you going? Don't move away,
I need you, your tears.

Don't make yourself run like that, I don't want
to bear this ancient guilt alone.

There will be time to go and then
do you really want to heal? It is late,

my lyre languishes for the useless struggle
with you, for this handful of laurels.

In the block of stone

In the block of stone I look for breath,
a pose, the old road.

If I move it part of it falls
— this is my challenge, I tempt fate.

Stay with the dead man

Stay with the dead man,
don't leave him.

Ready your hands,
you have to carve him.

Ten hours

I still have horas X, 20
ten hours, as is right.

Thrown

Thrown
into the warm earth

carelessly
heaped;

buried
in a lake of leaves:

I, old wager,
imprint, sediment.

On the waters

On the waters of the river you will float
tragic mask, obscene will.

You dared what you shouldn't have,
greedy for charms and new breaths,

eroded material, an excess of faith.

I fill the hourglass with dirt

I fill the hourglass with dirt.
I really want to stay
on this bank and slow down
the torment of my empty body,
of my old role.

There is no help for us in the night

There is no help for us in the night.
The last light has died, the sky is silent.

The waters flee full of regrets.
The gaze glides in the wind,

the step fades in distant echoes.
No skull passes, seen again.

No one will get through smoothly

No one will get through smoothly
between ruins and first moves.

In search of the last word
it's all a waste of energy,

food for the morgue,
held at the throat.

No respite

No respite, my skin exposed,
I fought my wounds.

I sought the perfect aim,
the path to open up, the sound.

Post talia dona I will be punctual, 21
I will rush to hide where I must.

Murmuring the old prayers
I will slam into the buried flesh,

in the grave that closes.

Between the eyes

The wound of conceit appears between the eyes
each time the boat sinks into the eddies

of the worldly desperation I need,
that I don't want. My veins explode and push

spilling more blood, seeking company.
Who will protect me from all this? I will be ready

to leave alone, as is right, ready for the fight,
to lick from the lips the pungent smell

of burials. From the depths of time
the abyss endlessly pours, this moment.

A shadow sparkles on the ancient sarcophagi

A shadow sparkles on the ancient sarcophagi,
its alacrity scorns its own fate.

It senses the untraceable, reflects the road.
It slows its breath: "let death come!

It will not stop my heart!" — it says
lamenting restive, trampling.

Let it go proud to the grave,
poet's body swollen with clouds.

At the bottom of the stone

At the bottom of the stone
new roads open up.

Sol me rapuit, 22
it took me far.

I no longer want to think,
only to spend one more day

beside you.
For once, to lose

the count, to forget
everything, to merge

into this heap of bones,
to fight shadows.

Captured by the contagion of the earth

Captured by the contagion of the earth,
I work on my plot in secret.

Someone has heard me,
wants to whisper it to the wind.

Life has not yet killed me.
I accept going out elated into the night,

I bark, spike, then return.
I need my den,

to breathe, to refresh myself.
I settle in among my infirm.

Howling they await my arrival.

The vortex sounds

Cito redditus umbris, 23
stuck in a distant harbor,

you fade away on the verge
of the cravings you lose hope.

The vortex
of deep veins sounds,

you prick up your ears,
in the hidden rooms,

you smell the remains of the will.
Guided by instinct

you try to flee, you look for
the travelled roads,

you correct the words.
nothing can be done: mors

inimica uenit, the ancestors' veil
falls quickly. 24

Dis Manibus 25

Dis Manibus.
Let me heal, go back to eating,
to seeing the light, the sea, things. That I may stop
imagining a script, may it quench the thirst,
desire, boredom. May you finally abandon
every ambition, this languid voice.
Do you really want me?
Not me. Not yet.

In fronte pedes XII, in agro pedes XVI

Breathless, the veins
no longer respond,

the deceptions stop breathing.
If you could get rid of time,

yearn for a new pitfall,
start again. Captured by worms,

without blood or pain you drown
hope, lose your way.

Tell me how to do it

Tell me how to do it
to turn away

to mingle with the earth,
to go slowly up in smoke.

A pool of mire

A pool of mire
ferments beneath the cross,
blossoms into a lament,
spreads in the night.

I ran away, hold me tight

Fugi, tene me, don't leave me. 26
Bare your breast for me, let me rest.

The vein writhes

The vein writhes,
the pressure increases,
it rises in the throat,
sprinkles the word.

I sew the hemorrhage

I sew the hemorrhage,
I know how to,
I'll put in
a new needle
to bark.

You dig where there's no oxygen

You dig where there's no oxygen,
where the echo is lost,
where the place is empty.

Tempt fate

Tempt fate,
finish the sentence,
perhaps someone
will come and save you.

Miserable land

ἀπὸ τούτου ἀγκῶνος 27
I will go away
to escape the envy
of a miserable land.

Ungrateful it will suck
from my mouth.

It will nourish my bones.

If I should die tonight

If I should die tonight
go to my room,

gather up all my things
run far away, make a bonfire of them.

You flay the bark shelter

You flay the bark shelter,
croak blood, rot away.

You awaken tense beneath the skin,
sharpen the blades, face the danger.

Your breastplate cracks the mirrors,
gathers images among the reflections.

Something has gone wrong

Something has gone wrong,
I'm not sure what but my old

armor is a little weaker today,
my throat breathes a cry of dust.

I draw the blade from my side.
The wound gurgles, it smells of incense.

It won't be glutted.

In the stream of pulses

In the stream of pulses
I found myself.

I let sink
a sketched image.

With its trickle
it stained the air,

flooded the rock,
fed the pool.

Do not stop it
It will continue to fall.

Open your eyes

Open your eyes.

The referee is upon you.
Everything is moving and you

can't get up.

Hoc est, sic est,
aliut fieri non licet. 28

This is the realm of the long shadows

This is the realm of the long shadows,
the empty faces. The gravity that hungers.

Don't make me speak

Don't make me speak. My throat bleeds invective.
My body is always writing the same page.

The closed maw of night burns with morning:
It is full of memories, voiceless, it swallows.

I will keep it safe, not allow it to open in public.
Let it bleed down there, on the high seas,

let it hold its tongue,
let it eat itself, go quickly to hell.

Look at my yesterday's wound

Look at my yesterday's wound,
my practice for death.

I opened it up again and was sated
in a pitiless night,

of buried muses, of regrets.
I've found a way out,

put my shadow behind me,
started on the main road.

Slumped in the scrub

Slumped in the scrub I feed on soil.
The forest all around shakes, seethes.

The branches gnaw at my flesh, they writhe,
they tighten their grip above me. The spirits

remember my gaze, they swarm.
They'll have a big party tonight.

I opened my body

I opened my body
to see better inside.

There is nothing in my breast:
only bones, flesh, veins

and blood, blood to waste.

The earth laughs at your fear of pain

The earth laughs at your fear of pain.
From its abyss it looks forward to a hot meal.

You lost your dreams in deep valleys,
you let them go in the mud of night.

Weary, you rush, you get up, you fall
little man, just a thing.

You put on your make-up at every change of scene

You put on your make-up at every change of scene,
you want to be ready.

You breathe deeply,
make your entrance as you should.

You've got a barrel pointed
at your throat,

you can't escape.
Light up your tongue,

to warm yourself sing,
withdraw into the night

then start again.
The curtain falls

into the bottom of the veins,
where you can't see.

Facing the wall

Facing the wall
the intestine weeps

gnawed by fear.
It writhes,

gasps, exhausted
in a runnel of pus

— it calls for a victim.

I pay dearly

I pay dearly for the words
you put into my mouth.

You fool me that I can see
the hereafter, to lose my way.

Your cry leaves me
only an empty gallery,

a longing for breath.

You will be remembered

You will be remembered for that line.
For that sculpted murmur?

Breathe water

Breathe water.
Is it a nightmare?
Or a safe haven?

I drag my bones

Under this light
I drag my bones.

Roll out the old adage:
"your head is hanging,

it is your root."
But deep down,

I don't believe it.
The earth

is calling me,
it opens up,

ignites.
It rots.

You are bruised

You are bruised:
your throat is slit,
the wound is open,
your mind is empty,
the air you breathe,
— dangerous.
Rest here,
back to the wall,
do not reply,
just count
the time that remains.

Out of focus

Out of focus the words
strike the break of day,
the tomb of my eyes.
I'm tired of dying
in the corner of a page.
I'd like to turn a leaf,
break off for a moment,
drag myself away from here.
I've had enough
of this stubborn desire,
of these marbles that weigh
on the pyre I've made for myself,
out of this whimsical wing.

You sunk your hands into your ribs

You sunk your hands into your ribs,
You went down into the depths of the veins.

You strangled words,
You hurt your ankles.

You targeted time
with your disguises,

your flags.

I am trapped in the scene

I am trapped in the scene:

Condemned to repeat
the remains of the night

I go over the broken memories again
and again, I sketch a count.

Our tears

Our tears
will streak the earth
with new roots.

Let's tighten our throats,
make them wrinkle.

The river has shaped a coffin

The river has shaped a coffin
for you, to give you shelter.

Let yourself go in that pallet,
sink like long ago,

as you remember.

It's not worth it

It's not worth going to war today,
getting hurt like this, embracing deception.

Punch after punch you slam into others,
with difficulty catch your breath, you suffer.

The night will charm the veins,
leave you in the warmth of the muses.

I don’t know how to go on

I don’t know how to go on,
I can no longer remember.

My throat is pressed
by a burnt crop,

a worn pattern.

I'm not talking about you

I'm not talking about you, not today,
actually hardly ever.

You ask me why
there's no reason if not that

the past is my door,
the only respite.

Off camera

Off camera the jaw scrapes,
it hits hard, chases the night,
brings me close to the dust.

The memory trickles

The memory trickles from your clenched neck,
from the noose drawn for you. You have no recollection,

but certainly hide this well. You slit your veins
with potions and curses, tore your arms,

erased the marks. Poet at rest you again
fall under the phial, attack the scene

composed by time.

You have brought me down here

You have brought me down here
where veins burn,

where rubble fills
my voice with promises,

where perhaps I am able
to see you.

Under the stone's feet

Under the stone's feet insomnia writhes.
A restless eye has emerged from the night's carcass.

It has opened in the breast to watch the day sink,
to strike the sky with its sound. It has swapped the light

for the dark to see and be hurt.

This is my body

This is my body
which starts, trembles

murmurs in the void.
It's mine, heavyweight

avid for pain.

Soiled with words I ruptured my veins

Soiled with words I ruptured my veins,
tied them, slit them and tore them out.

I hold fast, let my thoughts stutter,
let the world go on.

Why are you taking me away from this breath?

Why are you taking me away from this breath?
My head is throbbing, it has no peace.

You have cornered me,
nailed to an endless maze,

struck by pain. You don't stop seducing me
but the stage is worn, the actor stone.

He has been left breathless; on the threshold
he revels in grief for these lines

that run in fits and starts
— aimlessly.

What else?

What else?
Nil uolo, nil cupio 29

I breathe full throated,
I close my eyelids,

bury my wings.

It will be all or nothing!

It will be all or nothing!
Everything then, perhaps,
with these hungry worms
ready to chew the noose,
devour the breath.

View without eyes

View without eyes,
coffin of time,
ἀγρός, οἰκία,
κῆπος,
τάφος.

Your voice is counting down

Your voice is counting down,
falling into the void, scraping the shadows.

I cling to its echo,
I close my eyes, I absorb

its dross. I am used
to defeat,

it is a mere trifle.

This is how it will be

This is how it will be:
The coffin will be reflected

in the grey of the sky,
time will lose

importance,
the grass will caress

my face of stone.

Endnotes

1 *Or perhaps you were scared of it?*

From an inscription by Flavia Sophe. Inv. 40556 + 40662. Conserved in the Museo Nazionale Romano, Roma.

2 *My body is earth.*

3 *What is that that I see?*

4 *This road has such dust.*

5 *Alas.*

6 *I have been born many times*
but never like this.

I have altered and adapted the epigraph “Aliquoties mortuus sum, set sic nunquam,” “I have died many times but never like this” to: “Aliquoties natius sum, set sic nunquam,” “I have been born many times but never like this.”

7 *Shake your head, won’t you?*
Yet here you must go back.

8 *Now now.*
Immediately immediately.

9 *I plead with you, stone, to rest lightly on my bones.*

10 *You will find my names engraved in my epitaph.*

From Epitaffio in versi per un poeta. Inv. 29408. Lettere incise. Conserved in the Museo Nazionale Romano.

11 *Who are you?*
I am a stone.

Pebble inscribed in Oscan alphabet, 150–90 BCE. Inv. 247546. Conserved in the Museo Archeologico Nazionale di Napoli.

12 *I am nothing but a handful of ashes in a pyre on which to weep.*

From Epitaffio in versi per un poeta. Inv. 29408. Lettere incise. Conserved in the Museo Nazionale Romano.

13 *You amuse yourselves, I sing.*
From a fragment of painted plaster, Inv. 120031, Pompei, lettere dipinte in bianco. Conserved in the Museo Archeologico Nazionale di Napoli.

14 *I am amazed, o wall, that you have not fallen into ruins.*
From a fragment of painted plaster, Inv. 4706, Pompei, lettere graffite. Conserved in the Museo Archeologico Nazionale di Napoli.

15 *And yet I must go.*

16 "Coge mori," "Force me to die"
From a fragment of painted plaster, Inv. 4700, Pompei, lettere graffite. Held at the Museo Archeologico Nazionale di Napoli.

17 *Pay respect to those buried here along the public road.*
From an oval inscribed stele with representation of the deceased. Inv. 111434. End of VI century BCE. Early Sabellian dialect inscribed in a spiral around the figure. Conserved in the Museo Archeologico Nazionale di Napoli.

18 *Knife on the left, knife on the right.*

19 The Mole Antonelliana is a major landmark building in Turin, Italy named after its architect, Alessandro Antonelli. A *mole* in Italian is a building of monumental proportions.

20 (...) *10 hours.*
From an ossuary/altar, Inv. 72460, Roma, at the Porta Prenestina, letters in marble. Conserved at the Terme di Diocleziano, Museo Nazionale Romano.

21 *After such gifts.*

22 *The sun abducted me.*

23 *Quickly returned to the darkness.*

24 *Horrid death approaches.*

25 *To the Manes.*

26 *I ran away, hold me tight.*
From a necklace, Inv. 65043, letters engraved on bronze conserved at the Terme di Diocleziano, Museo Nazionale Romano.

27 "From this elbow"
"Ankon" is the name the Greeks gave the city of Ancona.

28 *This is what you see. It is like this.*
It can't be otherwise.

29 *I want nothing, desire nothing.*

30 *field, house, garden, burial.*
From a marble tablet, Roma. Cit. in *Epitaffi Greci* (Bompiani, 2019) 1148.

Author's Note

The inserts in Latin — where not specified in the notes — are taken from a selection of ancient epigraphic texts collected in the *Corpus Inscriptionum Latinorum*, Berlin 1863–1959, F. Buecheler, Carmina Latina Epigraphica, Leipzig 1895–1897, H. Dessau, *Inscriptiones Latinæ Selectæ*, Berlin 1892–1916.

The main source for the epigraphic collection at the Museo Nazionale Romano, is the Ministero per i Beni e le Attività Culturali Soprintendenza Speciale catalogue (Milan: Electa, 2012).

Regarding the epigraphic collection at the Museo Archeologico Nazionale di Napoli, reference is made to the Ministero per i Beni e le Attività Culturali Soprintendenza Speciale catalogue (Milan: Electa, 2017).

Thanks to Prof. Giusto Picone of Palermo University for comparing the translations that I have at times freely interpreted and adapted to the text.

Some epigrams were inspired by the Greek epitaphs collected by Werner Peek and those in the Antologia Palatina.

For the Greek, thanks to Monica Volcan, patient friend.

The poems "Gladiators," "The Seer," "Song of Love," and "Prodigal Son" were inspired by the works of the same names by Giorgio de Chirico.

The works by masters like Mantegna, Bramante, and Rosa were the activators of some of the poems in this collection.

Special thanks to Pierluigi Cerri, my first supporter, and to the directors James Bradburne (Pinacoteca di Brera), Fabrizio Masucci (Museo Cappella Sansevero), and Alfonsina Russo (Parco Archeologico del Colosseo) for having been valuable old-fashioned patrons over these years.

A recent recipient of the Montale Poetry Award, Gabriele Tinti is an Italian poet & writer. He has worked with the J. Paul Getty Museum, the Metropolitan Museum of Art, the British Museum, the Los Angeles County Museum of Art, the National Roman Museum, the Capitolini Museums, the Archæological Museum in Naples, the Ara Pacis Museums, the Colosseum and the Glyptothek of Munich, composing poems for ancient works of art, including *The Boxer at Rest*, the *Discobolus*, *Arundel Head*, the *Ludovisi Gaul*, the *Victorious Youth*, the *Farnese Hercules*, the *Hercules* by Scopas, the *Elgin Marbles* from the Parthenon, the *Barberini Faun* and many other masterpieces.

His poems have been recited by actors like Abel Ferrara, Marton Csokas, Kevin Spacey, Malcolm McDowell, Stephen Fry, Joe Mantegna, Michael Imperioli, Burt Young, Robert Davi, Jamie McShane, James Cosmo, Vincent Piazza, and Franco Nero.

In 2016 he published *Last Words* (Skira Rizzoli), a collection of found poetry in association with Andres Serrano.

In 2020 Tinti published *The Earth Will Come To Laugh and To Feast* (New York: Powerhouse Books), a poetry collection with illustrations by the artist Roger Ballen.

In 2021 he published *Ruins* (London: Eris Press).

COLOPHON

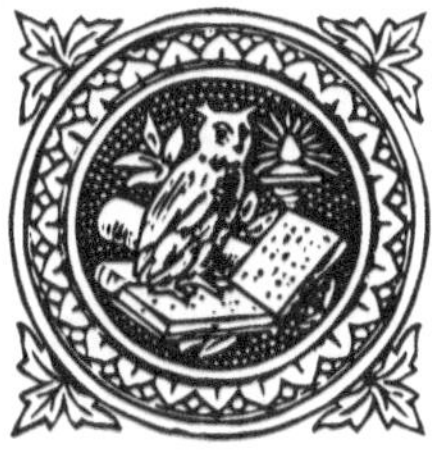

BLEEDINGS — INCIPIT TRAGOEDIA

was handset in InDesign CC.

The text font is *Warnock*.

The display font is *Ogg*.

Book design & typesetting: Alessandro Segalini

Cover design: CMP

Cover image: Andres Serrano, *Blood Stream*, 1987

BLEEDINGS — INCIPIT TRAGOEDIA

is published by Contra Mundum Press.

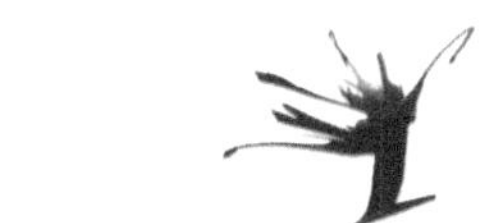

Contra Mundum Press New York · London · Melbourne

CONTRA MUNDUM PRESS

Dedicated to the value & the indispensable importance of the individual voice, to works that test the boundaries of thought & experience.

The primary aim of Contra Mundum is to publish translations of writers who in their use of form and style are *à rebours*, or who deviate significantly from more programmatic & spurious forms of experimentation. Such writing attests to the volatile nature of modernism. Our preference is for works that have not yet been translated into English, are out of print, or are poorly translated, for writers whose thinking & æsthetics are in opposition to timely or mainstream currents of thought, value systems, or moralities. We also reprint obscure and out-of-print works we consider significant but which have been forgotten, neglected, or overshadowed.

There are many works of fundamental significance to *Weltliteratur* (& *Weltkultur*) that still remain in relative oblivion, works that alter and disrupt standard circuits of thought — these warrant being encountered by the world at large. It is our aim to render them more visible.

For the complete list of forthcoming publications, please visit our website. To be added to our mailing list, send your name and email address to: info@contramundum.net

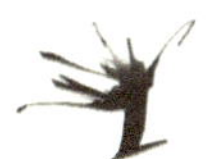

Contra Mundum Press
P.O. Box 1326
New York, NY 10276
USA

OTHER CONTRA MUNDUM PRESS TITLES

2012 *Gilgamesh*
Ghérasim Luca, *Self-Shadowing Prey*
Rainer J. Hanshe, *The Abdication*
Walter Jackson Bate, *Negative Capability*
Miklós Szentkuthy, *Marginalia on Casanova*
Fernando Pessoa, *Philosophical Essays*
2013 Elio Petri, *Writings on Cinema & Life*
Friedrich Nietzsche, *The Greek Music Drama*
Richard Foreman, *Plays with Films*
Louis-Auguste Blanqui, *Eternity by the Stars*
Miklós Szentkuthy, *Towards the One & Only Metaphor*
Josef Winkler, *When the Time Comes*
2014 William Wordsworth, *Fragments*
Josef Winkler, *Natura Morta*
Fernando Pessoa, *The Transformation Book*
Emilio Villa, *The Selected Poetry of Emilio Villa*
Robert Kelly, *A Voice Full of Cities*
Pier Paolo Pasolini, *The Divine Mimesis*
Miklós Szentkuthy, *Prae, Vol. 1*
2015 Federico Fellini, *Making a Film*
Robert Musil, *Thought Flights*
Sándor Tar, *Our Street*
Lorand Gaspar, *Earth Absolute*
Josef Winkler, *The Graveyard of Bitter Oranges*
Ferit Edgü, *Noone*
Jean-Jacques Rousseau, *Narcissus*
Ahmad Shamlu, *Born Upon the Dark Spear*
2016 Jean-Luc Godard, *Phrases*
Otto Dix, *Letters, Vol. 1*
Maura Del Serra, *Ladder of Oaths*
Pierre Senges, *The Major Refutation*
Charles Baudelaire, *My Heart Laid Bare & Other Texts*

2017 Joseph Kessel, *Army of Shadows*
Rainer J. Hanshe & Federico Gori, *Shattering the Muses*
Gérard Depardieu, *Innocent*
Claude Mouchard, *Entangled — Papers! — Notes*
2018 Miklós Szentkuthy, *Black Renaissance*
Adonis & Pierre Joris, *Conversations in the Pyrenees*
2019 Charles Baudelaire, *Belgium Stripped Bare*
Robert Musil, *Unions*
Iceberg Slim, *Night Train to Sugar Hill*
Marquis de Sade, *Aline & Valcour*
2020 *A City Full of Voices: Essays on the Work of Robert Kelly*
Rédoine Faïd, *Outlaw*
Carmelo Bene, *I Appeared to the Madonna*
Paul Celan, *Microliths They Are, Little Stones*
Zsuzsa Selyem, *It's Raining in Moscow*
Bérengère Viennot, *Trumpspeak*
Robert Musil, *Theater Symptoms*
Miklós Szentkuthy, *Chapter on Love*
Charles Baudelaire, *Paris Spleen*
2021 Marguerite Duras, *The Darkroom*
Andrew Dickos, *Honor Among Thieves*
Pierre Senges, *Ahab (Sequels)*
Carmelo Bene, *Our Lady of the Turks*
Fernando Pessoa, *Writings on Art & Poetical Theory*
2022 Miklós Szentkuthy, *Prae, Vol. 2*
Blixa Bargeld, *Europe Crosswise: A Litany*
Pierre Joris, *Always the Many, Never the One*
Robert Musil, *Theater Symptoms*
2023 Pierre Joris, *Interglacial Narrows*

SOME FORTHCOMING TITLES

Rainer J. Hanshe, *Closing Melodies*
Léon-Paul Fargue, *High Solitude*

AGRODOLCE SERIES ÆD

2020 Dejan Lukić, *The Oyster*
2022 Ugo Tognazzi, *The Injester*

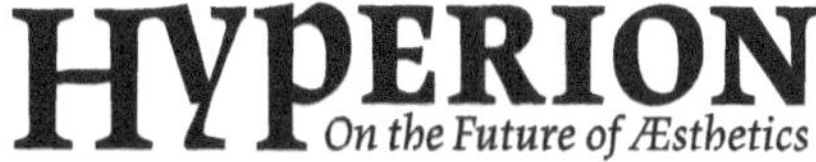

2006–2022

To read samples and order current & back issues of *Hyperion*, visit contramundumpress.com/hyperion

Edited by Rainer J. Hanshe & Erika Mihálycsa (2014 ~)

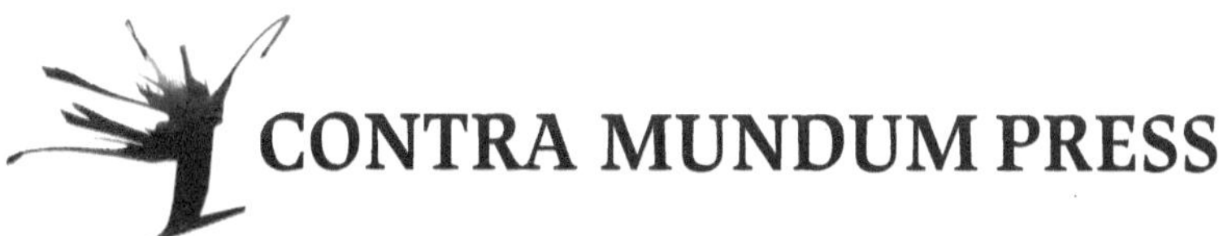

is published by Rainer J. Hanshe

Typography & Design: Alessandro Segalini

THE FUTURE OF KULCHUR
A PATRONAGE PROJECT

LEND CONTRA MUNDUM PRESS (CMP) YOUR SUPPORT

With bookstores and presses around the world struggling to survive, and many actually closing, we are forming this patronage project as a means for establishing a continuous & stable foundation to safeguard our longevity. Through this patronage project we would be able to remain free of having to rely upon government support &/or other official funding bodies, not to speak of their timelines & impositions. It would also free CMP from suffering the vagaries of the publishing industry, as well as the risk of submitting to commercial pressures in order to persist, thereby potentially compromising the integrity of our catalog.

CAN YOU SACRIFICE $10 A WEEK FOR KULCHUR?

For the equivalent of merely 2–3 coffees a week, you can help sustain CMP and contribute to the future of kulchur. To participate in our patronage program we are asking individuals to donate $500 per year, which amounts to $42/month, or $10/week. Larger donations are of course welcome and beneficial. All donations are tax-deductible through our fiscal sponsor Fractured Atlas. If preferred, donations can be made in two installments. We are seeking a minimum of 300 patrons per year and would like for them to commit to giving the above amount for a period of three years.

WHAT WE OFFER

Part tax-deductible donation, part exchange, for your contribution you will receive every CMP book published during the patronage period as well as 20 books from our back catalog. When possible, signed or limited editions of books will be offered as well.

WHAT WILL CMP DO WITH YOUR CONTRIBUTIONS?

Your contribution will help with basic general operating expenses, yearly production expenses (book printing, warehouse & catalog fees, etc.), advertising and outreach, and editorial, proofreading, translation, typography, design and copyright fees. Funds may also be used for participating in book fairs and staging events. Additionally, we hope to rebuild the *Hyperion* section of the website in order to modernize it.

From Pericles to Mæcenas & the Renaissance patrons, it is the magnanimity of such individuals that have helped the arts to flourish. Be a part of helping your kulchur flourish; be a part of history.

HOW

To lend your support & become a patron, please visit the subscription page of our website: contramundum.net/subscription

For any questions, write us at: info@contramundum.net

www.ingramcontent.com/pod-product-compliance
Lightning Source LLC
LaVergne TN
LVHW050959080826
845145LV00009B/2369